Jetiquette...
The Customer Experience and You

Gailen David

iUniverse, Inc.
New York   Bloomington

Jetiquette...The Customer Experience and You

iUniverse books may be ordered through booksellers or by contacting:

iUniverse
1663 Liberty Drive
Bloomington, IN 47403
www.iuniverse.com
1-800-Authors (1-800-288-4677)

ISBN: 978-0-595-49520-7 (pbk)
ISBN: 978-0-595-61135-5 (ebk)

Printed in the United States of America

iUniverse rev. date: 10/21/2008

Contents

First Serve Yourself

As I speak to audiences around the world on the subject of customer service (my award winning Jetiquette® program), I always reflect back on my personal journey and the lessons I have learned along the way. I believe we benefit from comparing stories about how changes in the ever-demanding arena of customer service affect us, regardless of our professional industry..

Becoming a flight attendant was not just an interest; it was a calling that began early in my childhood. At the tender age of nine, I was already an amateur travel agent. Armed with a notebook, a telephone, and an official Airline Guide, I began routinely booking airline trips for family and friends. It was more than child's play; from the beginning, I knew what I wanted to do.

I watched the movies. I knew what flight attendants did, and believed that their lives were full of adventure. They traveled to exotic locales and rubbed shoulders with the chic and trendy jet-set types who flew just for sport. They welcomed passengers, served coffee, vodka tonics, and the occasional meal, sympathetically tended to those afraid of flying, and fawned over the smaller passengers. They were gracious and polished, and I admired that in them. I actually used to wonder if they really had regular lives at all because they seemed so above the rest of us--almost immortal--as if their lives always took place above the clouds.

Even as a nine-year old, I knew air travel would be dreadful without flight attendants. A good cabin crew is invaluable to weary travelers. Who else can bestow upon them sweet nectar when they are thirsty, satisfying edibles when they are ravenous, and a pillow and blanket when they are exhausted? Flight attendants (and they look damn good doing it). Attractive, immaculate, and eager to please; that's what I wanted to be.

As I matured and prepared to enter the profession, I realized that flight attendants quite literally put their lives on the line for passengers every day. In an emergency, they are a passenger's first line of defense. And then, coincidentally, I learned that the first flight attendants were actually nurses who wore capes. So when I got my acceptance letter and stepped onto my first official flight with American Airlines, I felt like I had become a superhero.

I knew I was fortunate to work for such a great company. I was proud of my gold wings, starched shirt, and perfect tie. So proud, in fact, that I chose to wear my American Airlines T-shirt and socks on my days off. Sometimes, I even showed up at the airport a couple of hours before I had to, just so people could watch me walk around with my uniform on! I knew I was the embodiment of American Airlines, and I was proud to wear its symbols. When I occasionally heard coworkers complain about the job, I wondered, "How could anyone be unhappy doing a job like this?"

Believe it or not, however, my honeymoon with the customer service industry was short-lived. My initial sense of extreme pride turned to morbid disillusionment at the airline's service cuts, and I became personally insulted by what I interpreted as horrid customer conduct. As the "friendly skies" seemed to grow more and more turbulent, I grew increasingly disgruntled. I found myself trapped in an enormous air pocket of discontent.

If I was having a bad hair day, it was American Airlines' fault; if the passenger in 5B was talking on his cell phone instead of giving me his drink order, he was an inconsiderate jerk just trying to spite me. It seemed as though everyone I encountered was out to get me. I stopped looking at work as "me and the people" and viewed it more as "me and the enemy." I even suspected the company and passengers of secretly conspiring to make my life miserable. As a result, my internal motivation took a nosedive, and I took my frustration out on unsuspecting clients.

I actually began to bait and even publicly berate my customers. On one particularly stressful afternoon, I got on the airline's PA system and announced to the entire plane that we would all need to wait until a certain problem family got their act together before we could go about our business! This Gucci-draped family was more than a bit of a pain, and they were creating havoc in the cabin. Not prepared to handle them, I allowed myself to lose control.

In other instances, I developed and mastered a technique known as the Fly-By. If a customer did not respond to my requests appropriately, I made him pay dearly. I would hover just out of reach, pretending to be disinterested in the fact that he was talking on his cell phone or rooting through his carry-on bag. Then, when he noticed me and made a move to get my attention, I would simply "fly away," leaving him alone and bewildered. Then, to rub it in, I would periodically buzz past him, each time lingering just long enough to get his hopes up before taking off again.

What was I becoming? Yes, I was in need of a serious "altitude" adjustment.

My frustration and animosity for my professional issues spilled over into my personal life. I complained to anyone who would listen to me about the devil that was American Airlines and about its troupe of demon travelers who were out to cast me straight into the bowels of Hell. Eventually I crash-landed on a therapist's couch, with an extended layover in a reputable mental health facility. My personal wellbeing and my professional future were veritably up in the air.

Ten months later, after taking a leave of absence from the customer service industry and getting the help I needed, it dawned on me: while being emotionally invested in your profession is a good thing, investing in-- and feeding off--the wrong kind of emotion is not. And that's exactly what I had done at American Airlines. I had unknowingly surrendered to my employer every ounce of positive emotion that I possessed naturally at the age of nine.

Once I understood that about myself, I was able to actively work to get those positive emotions back. I knew I had to first serve myself if I hoped to ever effectively serve my clients again.

Take the Dare

In a sense, I took a critical look back in order to move forward. I wanted to regain the sense of purpose and satisfaction I'd felt as a child, so I looked back and tried to remember my sense of pride and power in a job well-done. It was then that I realized how much I really did love the job. I missed it. I missed the excitement and the diversity that traveling provided. I missed putting on a show for my customers. I missed the interaction with my coworkers.

Through all of this reflection, I slowly realized that I deserve to love what I do for a living, and I realized that the problems I'd encountered at American Airlines had come from inside me—not from the company or from the customers. Don't get me wrong: corporate leadership has a duty to its employees, but I could not wait for upper management at American Airlines to figure things out. I had a life to live! I decided to take full responsibility for my feelings so that I might regain a position of personal power. I, alone, was going to take control of my discontent. So, how was I going to turn this situation around? How could I be sure that the demons I'd created wouldn't come back to haunt me?

I returned to my career with a plan of action and a brighter frame of mind. If my "altitude" adjustment was going to stick, then I had to look at my job differently and have a new motivation for going to work. Rather than focusing on what my job was going to give me, I tried concentrating on how I could use my job to give to others. I wanted to have a positive affect on people that traveled on my flights, an affect that would buoy them up them for the rest of the day and beyond. Could I dare to make that much of a difference?

Fortunately, or maybe unfortunately, I discovered that I was not alone in my frustration. *One Foot Out the Door,* by Judith Bardwick, PhD, describes how such psychological recession is plaguing businesses everywhere. According to her book, a growing number of employees now report feeling emotionally absent from their jobs, if not completely then at least partially.

One Gallup Poll reported that 77 percent of Americans really dislike their jobs. Another reporting about employee engagement shows that about 17 percent of employees are so disengaged that they are actually trying to undermine their employers by running customers away, constantly complaining, or badmouthing their company at every opportunity.

A CareerBuilder.com survey revealed that 48 percent of retail workers did not look forward to going to work each day. So I realized that the phenomenon I experienced was not unique; there are other people out there feeling the same way.

With a volatile market forcing major downsizing, world-class companies are watching their reputations plummet faster than the Titanic. And, as morale hits all-time low, disgruntled, apathetic, underperforming, and even hostile service representatives are sending their customers packing. This is a mission-critical agenda for companies of all sizes and specializations: to get on board with a solid customer service initiative. It is possible to bring back an optimistic future in the public service industry, but to do so we've all got to make some changes.

Remember Jetiquette, the program I mentioned early on? It is a series of seminars and practical application tools I have created to reinforce positive customer service behavior.

I now, essentially, have two careers: I have an internationally recognized coaching business (Jetiquette received the 2008 Magellan Award from Travel Weekly Magazine), and I have returned to American Airlines as a purser. Once I had reconsidered what the airline industry meant to me, I happily returned to the first-class compartment, and am now providing impeccable service to CEOs, dignitaries, and the occasional celebrity. Back on the front lines, again experiencing the realities of the customer service industry, I can honestly say I love what I do for a living.

I deserve to love my job. I am worthy of this expectation. And so are you. Adopting this attitude about work makes it nearly impossible to create an "us vs. them" mentality. We must become better at doing our jobs, of providing quality response to customers' needs.

I see this as an opportunity. I take the dare.

Share the Territory

Quality customer service involves more than simply fulfilling a customer's request with a smile on your face. At its deepest level, exceptional customer service comes from an acute, inner sense of personal pride, from a willingness to accept an exalted level of responsibility for the customer's happiness. With the proper frame of reference, you can develop the interpersonal skills and survival strategies needed to provide the type of customer care that will seduce your guests.

But, wait a minute! You say you've worked in customer service for quite some time? You've seen it all? In the extreme, we bargain with impertinent, sometimes downright insolent, customers; with mollycoddled, boisterous children accompanied by clueless, egomaniacal parents; and even with the occasional rambunctious drunkard who spoils everyone's day.

Remember them, because you will probably have to deal with them again and again and again. They come with the territory—although, sometimes it's frustrating when they behave as though they own the territory, isn't it? I'll let you in on a secret: when you are cruising at Mach 0.8 in a flying tube, you have to share the territory; when you are ringing up a customer's order or checking her into her hotel room, you have to share the territory; when you are dealing with customer complaints and expectations, you have to share the territory.

When you share the territory, you are better able to appease even the most contrary customer by delivering the kind of service that lends dignity to your job. You must remember that the ability to deliver incredible customer service puts you in a position of tremendous power. You are in charge of another person's satisfaction.

Wow, how can you not love that kind of job?

Challenge Technology

People today are flying under largely different circumstances than those flying even just ten years ago. Our current obsession with technology has made it possible for travelers to literally forego physical interaction with other human beings. Cell phones, iPods, notebooks, and other personal electronic devices have changed the role of communication in society. And face it, isn't communication what customer service is all about? We used to rely on face-to-face contact and on well-developed interpersonal skills to accomplish our daily tasks. Not anymore. Right now, you could walk into any airport and board any plane, or enter almost any store and make any purchase, and not speak to a single person if you so choose.

We used to rely on mutual civility to get what we wanted. Now that we operate in this socially aberant era of technology, we think we don't *need* to be mutually civil—that is, until we *really* need something. While they might serve us in practical ways, cell phones, laptops, and iTunes at 30,000 feet are not going to provide the passenger in 15C with concrete customer care, with the beverage, the snack, or the pillow.

Care requires human interaction. It requires that we reach out to our customers on a meaningful level, and it is this meaning that inspires our customers to fly with us, to shop with us, to conduct any and all business with us again and again.

If you stop and think about it, the majority of our customers do not fit into the extreme hands-off category. Most customers are simply people going about their daily lives, trying to get from one place to the next as quickly, efficiently, and pleasantly as possible. No one (well, no one who is normal) goes out into this world thinking, "How can I turn this into the worst possible situation?" When we view our customers as people, similar to ourselves, it is harder to be brusque, and easier to love our jobs. Work to appreciate, and even to embrace, a wide variety of customer personality types, whether they are flying the friendly skies or standing with their feet firmly planted on the ground. You may be surprised to find that customers and service providers are strikingly similar in their desires: they both want human approval.

Really, don't we all want to turn off the technology sometimes and be human beings once in a while?

Stir the Pot

When you combine authentic service ingredients such as genuine interaction, personal connections, and congenial service, clients remember. Your customers are literally starving for a positive customer service experience. They crave the type of personal attention that touches them on a deep and meaningful level, that fulfills their inner needs. They are hungry for personal encounters that really matter and that satisfy their emotional famine.

As with fine cuisine, well-blended quality service elements create an experience your customers won't be able to resist. Your patrons will come to eagerly anticipate the "buffet" you've prepared for them and, once they have a taste of your service , they will dig right in. Authentic ingredients are amazing tools at your disposal. It doesn't matter in what order they are combined, because they will keep your customers coming back for second, third, and fourth helpings.

If you look at the pyramid below, you'll see that cordiality and personal connection are crucial to your recipe for successful customer service, and are based on the much larger practice of genuine interaction. Genuine interaction colors and shapes the biggest part of the overall customer experience, because it covers a wide range of behaviors and invokes a smorgasbord of positive emotions.

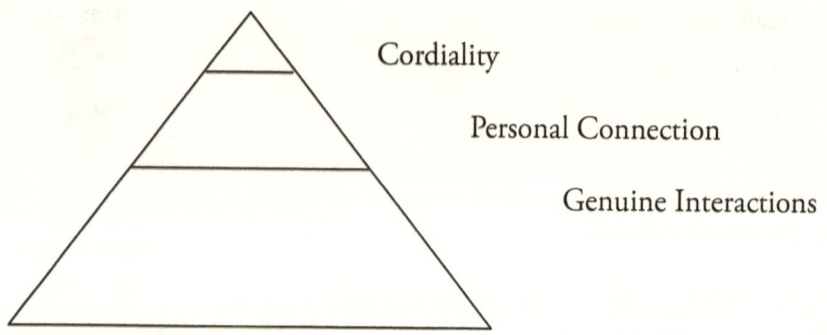

Cordiality

Personal Connection

Genuine Interactions

Serve your clients with sincerity, and remember: regardless of your rapport with a repeat customer, do not assume that he is automatically a satisfied customer. Attention must be paid, as the saying goes. The pot must always be stirred.

Be the Glue

As a general rule, human beings can smell a fake encounter a mile away. You could almost say it's encoded in our DNA, because it's reflected in the curve of our lips over our teeth when we smile, the tension in our handshake when we touch, and the meeting or aversion of our eyes when we greet another. In his book, the *A Psychology of Light*, Dr. Howard Teich discusses this phenomenon and how genuine interactions feed our most primal desire to be cared for, nurtured, and valued.

The primitive societies of Early Man revolved around hunting and gathering to meet basic human needs. Early Man formed working groups for efficiency, and instinctually hung together to protect those groups. However, as he learned to attend to his physical needs for food, clothing, and shelter, he began to understand the benefit of social interaction, both for pleasure and personal gain. As social interaction fed Early Man on an emotional level, tribes were formed in which humans built incredible reciprocal bonds of service, devotion, and care-giving, the glue of all societies since.

Today, even with our abundance of modern technology, people still understand the benefits of creating bonds that unite the human race in unique ways. Nowhere is this more evident than in the customer service and business industries, in which reciprocity can either make or break a union.

Successful CEOs, corporations, supervisors, and managers understand the value of forming a "tribe" in the workplace. These leaders recognize that productivity and job satisfaction increase when employees feel they are valued members of a team, united in a common goal. When people work together for the benefit of the tribe, efforts are organized, work gets done efficiently, turnover rates are low, productivity soars, and the customers benefit from a healthy business environment.

Unfortunately, many inattentive employers have experienced the peril and regret that comes from an "every man for himself" attitude.

Define Customer Service

By its very nature, the customer service industry prohibits any successful business from existing in a bubble. To fully understand the essence of customer service, you must understand the big picture. By itself, the word *service* has a positive connotation. It conveys a sense of willingness, of providing help before a request is even made. If you consider that service is defined as a "contribution to the welfare of others", you begin to realize that it is impossible for service to be a solitary endeavor. It is the human component in the world that maximizes and essentially guarantees long-term corporate success.

At its core, the customer service industry cannot rely on fancy gimmicks and competitive pricing. These components may get people in the door, but they won't guarantee repeat business because they aren't "real." Bells and whistles have their place in the consumer industry, but any schlep can blow a whistle or ring a bell (and even look good doing it). At some point, though, it doesn't take long for the customer to realize that most businesses dance the same dull dance to the same tired tune.

So it takes something special to develop a loyal customer following; this special something is the authentic human component.

The authentic human component is not limited to the employee-customer relationship; it extends far beyond. For example, it's risky to believe the fallacy that happy, professionally satisfied, loyal employees perform to the best of their abilities without a united tribe standing strong and tall behind them. Employees require genuine interaction on a daily basis as much as customers do. If you want your employees to consistently provide the customer and your company with the best they have to offer, then you must feed and nurture their emotional needs, as well.

Be the Model

If you are a leader, consider getting to know those you lead on a personal level. Just as wise and successful corporations tap into the power of genuine interaction with their customers, so too must they engage in genuine interaction with their employees. Find out what makes your employees tick on a personal level. How well do you know the people you supervise every day? Do they have families? What hobbies do they enjoy? What do they do outside the workplace?

When employers take the time to get to know their employees as people, a tribe begins to shape. Employees now feel valued and respected, and this validation and respect is communicated and transferred to the customer it is their job to serve.

Getting to know your employees motivates them and increases productivity. Motivated and productive employees have an internal desire to perform at their optimal levels, and this type of inspiration comes only from a place of emotion. Outstanding corporations have learned to tap into the psyches of their employees through genuine employee-management interaction. As a supervisor or manager, how can you expect your employees to practice what you preach if you do not practice it yourself? Treat your employees in the same manner with which you expect them to treat your customers.

When your employees arrive to work each day, greet them with a genuine smile, firmly shake their hand, and look them directly in the eye. This says, "Welcome, I'm happy to see you. I value what you have to offer the company today and every day." Thank your employees for their efforts and contributions. Show them in concrete ways that they are valuable to the corporation and that you appreciate them. You function as a powerful role model. Employees look to you for guidance with respect to how they should behave toward the customer and toward one another.

Like the customer, employees judge their superiors based on first impressions. They evaluate and rank you according to your physical appearance, your demeanor, and your level of professionalism, and the opinion they form invokes an emotional response within them. Beyond first impressions, when management feeds their employees on an emotional level, workers are satisfied on a primal level. They no longer come to work simply to collect a paycheck, but because they *want* to. Like the customer, they come into your place of business because it *feels* good to do so.

Correct Constructively

Employees are going to make mistakes because they are human. Just remember that each mistake is an opportunity for growth, personally and professionally. As a supervisor, you have the opportunity to make or break the situation when unfortunate instances arise. You are the greatest influence on your employees, and thus very powerful when mistakes occur. Remember to use your emotional intelligence, expertise, and professionalism to guide your employees through troubled waters.

Use setbacks as a way to humanely educate your employees about the needs of everyone involved. Most employees truly want to do a good job, and you provide a system of support when employee morale is low.

Get Personal

Genuine interactions work wonders in the customer service industry. When used appropriately, genuine interactions can set your company up for a long-term, mutually beneficial relationship with your customers. Again, it all boils down to the human factor. Human beings are emotional creatures and may respond to genuine interactions in a variety of ways, according to the specific circumstance.

A sincere smile and a heartfelt greeting set the tone for each customer service encounter. When a customer sets foot into a service industry, they want to feel welcomed; after all, the word "service" implies assistance provided willingly, and conjures up comforting images of needs being met. Service that is rendered with a begrudging attitude is not service at all; as a result, it is crucial that the customer's first impression be a positive one.

This initial encounter should meet and ideally exceed the customer's expectations, put everyone at ease, and make the customer feel like he has come to the right place. Do you really understand how valuable you are to your customers? In his book, *Chocolates on the Pillow Aren't Enough*, Jonathan Tisch, chairman and CEO of Loews Hotels, describes how it does not take extreme rudeness to drive away a customer. An astounding 68 percent of customers have claimed to have left a company simply because of ambivalent treatment[2]. Who among us chooses to do business where we have been ignored?

Genuine encounters are invaluable when a product or service does not meet a customer's expectation. When customers find themselves frustrated or even angry with their customer experience, genuine encounters can help make things right again. When an employee or company apologizes for an unforeseen pitfall, the customer is encouraged to accept the fact that the situation was regrettable and unintended. It serves to diffuse the situation because, really, what can you say when someone offers a sincere apology and then sets out to make amends and provide restitution? This validates the customer's angst, and it lets her know the company is on her side and understands the situation from her point of view.

Get Connected

Personal connection draws the employee and the customer together because it opens a common door. A personal connection can be something as little as asking, "How are you doing today?" When asked with sincerity, and topped with friendly eye contact and a firm handshake, this simple question provides the opportunity for meaningful dialogue between both parties. Inconspicuously, a door has been opened, a bridge has been built, and a relationship has been established. "It's the people-to-people connections, regardless of price point, that differentiate a customer's experience," says David Neeleman, founder of JetBlue Airways[3].

Personal connection tells others that you are interested in them and their lives. Noticing family photos in a client's wallet or skis on the roof of his car provides a window into the private world of people who would otherwise remain strangers. If done with professionalism and sincerity, complimenting the customer in subtle ways lets her know you have cared to notice. This is what we all really want: to be welcomed into the lives and activities of other people.

These are all relatively effortless ways to make a meaningful personal connection, and they not only stay with people, but also ultimately impact subsequent personal encounters throughout the day. Perhaps even more important, making a personal connection simply feels good. When you send out good vibes to others, you often see them reflected directly back at you.

Do Unto Others

Cordiality is the idea that we should treat others as we wish to be treated. Everyone deserves respect, courtesy, and kindness. Cordiality is critical in our modern technological era. It is easy to neglect interpersonal communication skills. We've got the Internet, e-mail, and text messaging and this makes it easy to relegate face-to-face communication to second-class citizen status; however, this ideology is a huge mistake in the world of customer service.

Cordiality is the obligation of every person on the planet today, because it sets an admirable example for those around you, and you never know who is listening or watching. You never know who is going to be impacted by what you do or say. We owe it to one another to be civil and polite. Nothing positive comes from being impertinent; in fact, that only serves to perpetuate hostility, frustration, and anger. Remember my Fly-By?

We all learned the basic rules for civilized society by the time we had graduated from Kindergarten, right? At a bare minimum, we should say "please" when we want something, "thank you" when something is given to us, and "I'm sorry" when we have hurt someone. These seemingly insignificant gestures can make all the difference in the world, because they are ways of letting others know we appreciate and value them.

We all wish to be treated with respect. Make it your goal to personally do so unto others.

Be a Close Encounter

An acquaintance and I were chatting recently about her decision to buy a new car. I was interested to learn about her encounters with the dealership salespersons.

Dealer #1: The salesperson was all right; he wanted to sell me a new Subaru Outback for $26,800. He was polite, but with his rumpled clothes and flyaway hair he looked as though I had interrupted his afternoon nap. He didn't remember me from one visit to the next. His price quotes were disorganized, and when he found out that I was unwilling to purchase the vehicle immediately--I told him I needed time to think about his offer—he lost interest in me and wandered off, presumably to finish his nap. I don't believe he ever did actually introduce himself.

Dealer #2: Dave was always polite and happy to see me. He remembered my name each time I came in for a test drive. Furthermore, Dave called me periodically, although he never pressured me, to see how I was progressing in my decision-making process. After some negotiating, he said he could sell me the same car for $27,200. His best offer was a full $400 higher than Rumplesuit's.

My seven-year-old son is in love with Subarus, especially their little sporty model. During each trip to the dealership he would sit inside the car, pretending to drive. One day Dave showed up with a set of Subaru keys just for my son. Needless to say my son was impressed, but so was I. Later, Dave ordered a toy model Subaru in the same sporty style my son adored. Keep in mind that I had not settled on a car at this point. I had in no way committed to the purchase of a vehicle, but nevertheless my family and I were being treated as though we were something special.

Ultimately I spent the extra $400 dollars and bought the Subaru from Dave. I didn't buy it from him because of the keys or the toy that he gave to my son. I bought the car from Dave because of how he made me feel.

He respected my decision to consider his offer, and did not lose interest in me when I did not make an impulsive purchase. He was kind, he remembered my name, and he did not pressure me. He paid attention to my family and took an interest in us on a personal level. In my opinion it was $400 well spent, and I will return to this particular dealer for my future automotive needs, specifically because of Dave.

Well, how do you possibly find fault with a decision like that? This story made my day.

Stand on Common Ground

All people have certain expectations. We expect to be taken seriously, we expect to be heard, and we expect to get what we paid for. Just as importantly, we expect courtesy and civility as a natural part of human interaction. Do you really think your customers are all that different from you? When you get to know the needs and emotions of your patrons, it is hard to separate them from yourself, because you can see yourself in them. The lines between the "us and them" become blurred. In fact, we stand on the same side of the line and become ... the "we" team.

Think of a really great customer service encounter you have experienced. Imagining yourself as the customer, what are some adjectives you can think of to describe it? Do words like genuine, courteous, knowledgeable, understanding, and empathetic come to mind? Notice that these adjectives conjure up images of action as well as feeling. Actions are great, but actions that leave positive, lasting impressions are the most powerful, and will ensure you are remembered in the hearts and minds of not only your customers, but also fellow human beings in general.

Emote

Many companies falsely believe that low prices and special offers keep customers loyal; however, customer satisfaction and customer loyalty are two very different animals. If I'm hungry, I can eat a hamburger. I can pretty much eat a decent, reasonably priced hamburger anywhere and walk out the door feeling satisfied on a physical level. However, if I go to a place that has a fantastic atmosphere and employees who connect with me on a personal level, leaving me feeling physically *and* emotionally full, you can bet I'm going to return there, even if I've got to pay a bit more than I would at its competitor's. I'm going to return because my emotional self remembers the positive human connection. My inner being craves this type of satisfaction as much as I physically crave that burger.

In other words, if you want to move beyond customer satisfaction and into the territory of customer loyalty, you've got to invest some emotional labor into the mix. You've got to see through the customer's eyes and walk in the customer's shoes. You've got to engage customers on both a physical and emotional level. Physically getting them through the door is the easy part; establishing an emotional connection and lasting relationship can be trickier. It's trickier because you've got to make yourself vulnerable by taking the first step and revealing the emotional side of yourself. You've got to entice them by looking them in the eye and prompting authentic conversation. You've got to be genuinely happy to see them. You've got to actively listen to them, communicate clearly, and be ready to handle their complaints and concerns.

You have been entrusted with a powerful responsibility, and you need to have a strategy in place in order to be successful.

Allow Them Importance

THE OLD GAILEN:

Part of the first-class experience is boarding the aircraft before all of the other passengers, taking that comfortable leather seat, and getting a predeparture beverage from the flight attendant. It's often not an easy job for the flight attendant to complete this service before the door closes, and little annoyances can slow things down even further.

One of these annoyances is the cell phone. Some passengers in first class like to get right on their cell phones as they take their seats, spilling out multi-million dollar figures and major league business deals for all to hear. Well, the Old Gailen used to get so incredibly irritated by the "cell phone people," as I called them, because when I would approach them with an offer for a preflight cocktail or beverage, I could not get their attention--they were too involved in their cell phone conversations.

I developed a way of dealing with this. I called it the three-second rule. When I approached one of these people, he or she would have three seconds in which to respond. (Actually, they had less than that, because I often started counting on two.) So if they did not give me their attention by the time I reached three, the window of opportunity slammed shut. I would disappear.

My next ploy would be to let the rest of the crew know that they were not to get this passenger anything for the entire flight. He was *mine* and became the object of my "affection" for the rest of the trip. So then, what passive-aggressive behavior did I display for the remainder of the trip? Well, in addition to my notorious Fly-By routine, here's one I used on a particular woman that committed a cell phone infraction:

Baiting—This technique really put my theatrical skills to work. I would go to the area where the punished passenger was sitting and pretend that I was busy with little in-flight duties: open an overhead bin and peak inside, maybe shift some luggage around or rearrange some pillows and blankets, all the while within inches of this unfortunate passenger. I could feel her anticipation building as she truly thought she would be able to get my attention. Sadly, the moment she would begin to say, "Excuse me … " I would slam the overhead bin shut and blast off again, leaving her crushed and disillusioned.

I have to admit that it was pretty fun. But was this really working for anyone? Well it certainly was not working for this poor passenger!

And I must tell you that this was not working for me either. I would leave a situation like this actually feeling like I had failed. I realized that I had also ignored people providing services to me and it was completely unintentional. Their reactions were different than mine. Rather than do all of those things that I

23

did to punish me, they would just smile and continue. This type of reaction actually got my attention as I was so pleased with the way I was being treated as a customer. I am very grateful that I was able to see this so that I could start making some changes to my attitude.

THE NEW GAILEN:

I knew I had to rethink this whole approach to difficult customers for two reasons: their offenses were really not unforgivable; and I knew from experience that difficult customers will always be there. I realized I couldn't change that. So rather than try to change the world, I decided it was time to change myself.

After my leave of absence, I came back to work ready to try to do things differently, but I was not completely confident that I'd be able to do so successfully. What would I do when I encountered the situations that used to set me off? Well, it did not take long to find out.

On my first day back to work, there he was: a gentleman passenger in my first-class cabin on his cell phone. I said to myself, "Gailen, just stay calm. Get yourself together and show this guy a little patience. He is another human being simply trying to get things done. It's not personal, and he is not trying to irritate you." I reached his row as he continued his conversation and I just waited silently. He soon noticed me (it took over three seconds, but that was okay) and he asked his caller to hold.

"Hi," he said to me.

"Hello sir, I'm sorry to interrupt your call. I just thought you might want a beverage before take-off," I said with a smile.

"Sure, I'll have a vodka tonic." Well, I knew before he said it that he wanted a vodka tonic, because that seems to be the drink of choice for all first-class passengers.

As I turned to get his cocktail, I heard him return to his conversation and say something interesting. "Sorry about that, it was the first-class flight attendant asking me if I would like my first-class beverage. I am in first-class."

It was at that moment that I realized that part of giving customers "the experience" is making them feel important. I had played a major part in giving this passenger an ego boost. The Old Gailen would have never allowed that to happen.

On that day, the New Gailen decided to add "making people feel important" to my list of favorite job responsibilities.

Pass the Sugar

Picture this: what reaction will you get if you approach a customer with a furrowed brow and sour lips, and mumble, "Yeah, what can I getcha'?" Do you think you might get off on the wrong foot? At the least, you'll make a horrific first impression, and at the worst you'll inspire the customer to take you down a peg by being hostile, annoying, or needy. You'll elicit an emotional response all right, but not the kind that will help you on a personal or professional level; you've just let your customer know in no uncertain terms that they are a fly in your soup. You've made it crystal clear that you have better things to do, or more important people to spend your time with.

On the other hand, let's look at another approach. What if you consciously open your dialogue with a genuine "how are you today?" and then actually wait for the customer's response? What a novel idea! Don't ask someone how they are doing if you can't take the time to, or are not interested in, hearing their answer. Trust me, because I've been there: it's all in the attitude!

Moods spread like Avian Bird Flu. If the next customer in line hears you pleasantly engaging with the stranger ahead of him, it prepares him emotionally for his encounter with you. If you approach every customer with an authentic desire to please and care, no matter how unpleasant he may look, I guarantee that you will diffuse any negative vibes. Voila! That means an easier job for you, and a satisfying experience for the customer.

A simple greeting, a genuine smile, and a sincere "thank you" go a long way. Have you really thought about the potential benefits and long-term consequences of accommodating every customer in an extra-special way? When you do this consistently, your customers are often publicly grateful. They may be so impressed that they send a heartfelt testimonial, spreading the word personally about their positive experience with you and the industry you work for. As a result, you and the company receive loads of positive press because of your random acts of civility, kindness, and care.

When you see your customers as allies rather than enemies, a whole new world opens up for both of you. Your customers are real people with real feelings and real expectations. It is unbelievably satisfying to not only meet, but also to exceed customer expectations, and the rewards that result extend far beyond the confines of your immediate encounter.

As my dad always says, you catch more bees with honey than with vinegar, and nowhere is that saying more applicable than in the customer service industry.

Be Random

You've heard of the Butterfly Effect? The Butterfly Effect is the scientific theory that we exist in a system of chaos. It supports the idea that seemingly miniscule changes to this chaotic system, applied in specific ways, bring about enormous change. In the context of your job as a customer service professional, the Butterfly Effect begins with a single, positive human interaction based on an act of random kindness.

What happens next is based on a variety of factors; however, imagine the potential for a positive outcome. You could say that it simply feels good to present yourself as a professional and to have a positive encounter with someone else. You could also say that self-satisfaction comes from doing the right thing: for example, treating a customer with respect and courtesy, and doing it well.

If you have affected this customer in a positive manner, news will spread faster than a tornado through a trailer park. After all, the most logical outcome is that this customer will spread the word to others about your exceptional customer service, which means that you have increased the likelihood that this customer will return to your place of employment. You have also increased the odds that the good news will make it to your employer.

Imagine the immense feeling of satisfaction you'd get by learning that word had spread about something exceptional that YOU did? There truly is nothing more fulfilling, and it begins with a single moment. This Butterfly Effect is what makes working in customer service so incredibly worthwhile. You deserve this. You deserve to love what you do—now, tell me you don't feel powerful in your job.

Count On Yourself

The even better news is that it doesn't stop there. Another benefit: there will come a time when you feel ready to ask for a pay increase. Maybe the cost of living has gone up, or life is requiring you to take on serious responsibilities that prompt you to aspire to a higher salary. When that time comes, you will have the confidence and the success statistics to back yourself up.

In short, when your group's customer service ratings are consistently strong, it's easy to justify a pay increase. You are in a position of power because your services are in greater demand. Employers recognize that in today's society, a proven track record of exceptional customer service is money in the bank.

As an added bonus, there may come a time when you choose to move toward other employment options. When you do, you'll have a leg up, because a proven customer track record will follow you by way of business references and letters of recommendation. Over time, your professional history will simply speak for itself.

Do you realize the untapped power you have as a customer service professional? You are the face and the voice of the company, the billboard and the megaphone that can make or break a business, the person that can cause a positive ripple effect because of your kindness.

Everything that happens between the company and the customer filters through your conscientious words and actions. That is an extremely powerful position to be in!

If you think about it, exceptional customer service also has a selfish side, and that is definitely okay. There literally *is* something in it for you if you do it right. Seeing a customer's expression of satisfaction when you've connected with her and ably provided her with an exceptional customer experience is a priceless payoff unto itself. And if a company has a program to recognize top performers, monetarily or otherwise, all the better.

Belong

Do you belong to a worker's union? Even if you don't, you know about this phenomenon, or have at least likely heard it before: there is power in numbers. Remember the glue?

If you want to cement your position of power as an employee even more, team up with your colleagues, and you will be twice as effective. You and your coworkers share a common bond by working toward a common goal, so use colleagues as allies in your customer service mission.

Your coworkers can be a great resource on multiple levels because they are a fountainhead of positive feedback and encouragement. They know how hard you work every day, because they are in the same boat. They share not only your triumphs, but your setbacks as well.

Coworkers can also be great teachers. Use more experienced coworkers as mentors. Just as importantly, see yourself as a role model for those coming into the job behind you.

When you work together as a cohesive unit something magical happens: people use their heads to solve problems, and every team member begins to view his or her role as unique and essential to the long-term vision.

It's at this point that excellent customer service starts to go beyond the professional, and joins together fellow employees on a personal level. There is no "me," "you," or "them." In this sense, you benefit personally *and* professionally when you see your colleagues as a support system. Everyone on the team shares a common bond through experience.

When each person on your team radiates cordiality, civility, and competence, customers can't help but revel in it. Because it is irresistible, they turn to putty in your hands. Your customers are happy because their needs are being met. They feel as though they are understood and cared for because they are treated with kindness and respect. On top of that, your employers are happy because they're pulling in more revenue. The positive attitude, whether transferred from employee to customer, customer to customer, or employee to employee, is contagious, and as a result, the company outperforms the competition.

And ultimately—whether it be in the form of customer gratitude, a sense of accomplishment, a more pleasant working environment, or a personal feeling of belonging to something larger—it all comes back to you.

Be Your Own Best Ally

This is not a pretty story, but one many of my colleagues and I know all too well:

I was working first class on a flight from LAX to O'Hare a few years ago. My section included a mother travelling alone with her ten-year-old son. I was making my rounds, taking drink orders when I came to their row. I began with the child.

"What can I get for you, sweetie?"

"I want a Coke," he replied.

Speaking to the boy as I would my own son, I said, "What's the magic word?"

Without missing a beat, the mother leaned over and responded, "Oh, honey, you don't have to say 'please' to her."

I wasn't sure how to respond. I felt very angry and saddened. I wanted to refuse service to both of them for being so condescending. How could a mother educate her child this way? I took it personally and I wanted to get even. I made a judgement about that mother right there on the spot, but I bit my tongue, took her drink order and then ignored them for the rest of the flight. Why should I lift a finger for people like that?

This is just one example of how thankless this job can be. Apparently the woman complained about me, and I received a letter of reprimand in my file. This woman and her child were blatantly disrespectful, yet the company sided with them over me. I fumed for days about this single act of inconsideration.

Do you feel like yours is a thankless job? If you are feeling down about working in customer service, you are not alone. When you feel this way, though, just remember that your company has entrusted you with an amazingly important responsibility. They rely on you to represent them to the public, to speak and act on their behalf. This is a great privilege.

It can be tempting to let a bad day at work take its toll on our emotions, self-esteem, or ego. Often we wind up feeling misunderstood, unappreciated, resentful, or even hostile. Sometimes this can be due to company cutbacks, supply and demand, or an unfortunate series of events. Perhaps that customer walked into a given situation with the expectation of an intended outcome; they did not come with the intention of judging you as an individual.

Ultimately, these trying times require you to do your job to the best of your ability and to conduct yourself in the most professional manner possible. Do what you need to do to feel happy, confident, capable, productive, and amicable. Begin to acknowledge all the wonderful ways you enhance the lives of others every day!

For example, if the purchasing experience of the customer was a complete disaster, you could potentially be the singular bright spot in the overall experience, depending on the demeanour you present.

In other words, recognize situations like these for what they truly are: unfortunate and at times unavoidable, nothing more. When you are blindsided by negative experiences on the job, it is most important to remember: do not take the negatives personally. You are not the one who created the weather delay. You did not build or maintain the aircraft that needs an extra hour of mechanical attention. You can, however, take control of the situation and keep the peace.

Be Empathetic

Unconditional love and support comes from family and friends; love and support with strings attached comes from working in the customer service industry. You should feel powerful given the fact that, frequently, you are the one pulling many of those strings.

You will encounter many different personalities as you fly your own version of the friendly skies. And yes, that can sometimes include cantankerous and unreasonable individuals. Don't be shy about communicating a need for assistance in difficult customer service situations. If you are new to the business and have little experience in dealing with stubborn, outspoken, or even cruel customers, watch and learn how other employees handle the situation.

In trying times it helps to take a deep breath and emotionally step back from the situation. It also helps to muster up some sympathy, (yes, you heard me correctly), for the seemingly abrasive customer. What could possibly be so wrong in this individual's life that he actually *chose* to represent himself in this manner? Even these difficult characters are worthy of your respect and sympathy, if for no other reason than to keep yourself from being dragged down with them into the depths of despair!

Through time, you'll grow that thick skin that others in the customer service industry can relate to. And you can learn to tame even the most unruly passenger by adopting a few simple tricks of the trade.

Use Emotional Intelligence

Customers and employees alike have two sides of their brains working simultaneously. Both have an emotional side, which deals with impulses, creativity, and feelings. Both also have a logical side. This side wishes to categorize situations and apply reason to everything.

How does this relate to customer service? When an unhappy and seemingly inconsolable customer or co-worker is making things unbearable, your first instinct may come from that emotional side of your brain. You may want to yell and scream, punch something, or perhaps plot subtle, yet hostile, revenge against the person contributing to your unhappiness. Are there better ways to handle the situation?

When emotions like these surface, remember to keep your cool and save that energy for kickboxing class or the next time you talk to your ex. For now, tap that amazing power and energy, and use it for something constructive—otherwise you run the risk of taking a bad situation and making it worse.

This is called being emotionally intelligent. Regardless of industry, people at the top of their fields are more than just good at their profession. They are more than personable, creative, intuitive, and resilient. They've got more going on below the surface than many would imagine; you can bet that they are emotionally intelligent.

The ability to use your emotional Intelligence (EI) in the workplace can potentially make or break your professional career. Your Emotional Quotient (EQ) is the ability to recognize and monitor your own thoughts, feelings, and emotions as well as you can monitor those of others. Exceptional people use their emotional intelligence to guide their actions, and reactions, in a variety of situations.

EQ is different than an IQ. A person's IQ measures "brain smarts" and it is relatively static, meaning it does not change much over time. While there is some debate over the potential fluctuation of EQ over time, many believe EQ can be learned, shaped, and improved upon through time and training. In fact, many companies are actively seeking ways to test, nurture, and use the emotional intelligence of their employees to increase revenue and productivity. Employers of major corporations are realizing that cognitive skills can get a qualified candidate in the door, but emotional intelligence is what is going to help that employee flourish and advance within the ranks of the company which is covered at length in a very interesting book by Daniel Coleman, *Working with Emotional Intelligence.*

Imagine that as you walk through the airport terminal on the way to your flight, you make eye contact with others. You exchange smiles and an occasional "hello" or "good morning" while walking past the ticket counters and to the security line. A confused passenger stops right in front of you, looking around, appearing lost. Rather than walking around her, you ask if she needs assistance, and then you patiently listen to her reply. You then politely direct her to the correct concourse and wish her a pleasant trip.

You can now continue on your way, knowing that you just helped someone. As you pass through security, you give a smile and ask how the often-unappreciated TSA representative's day is going. He smiles back at you with gratitude because you cared enough to ask.

By the time you reach the harried gate agent and greet him with a smile, you have already had a handful of positive interactions that have gotten your day off to a fantastic start. You've also added a bright spot to the day of those you've come in contact with. You've made a difference by understanding what others may be going through and reacting accordingly.

Wouldn't it be nice if every work day started like this? The truth is that days like this don't always just happen. Our ability to influence the quality of our daily experiences on a moment-by-moment basis is the key to creating our desired realities. Each human interaction we have during the course of a day requires us to make split-second decisions regarding our perceptions and responses.

Since our careers are built on interactions with customers and coworkers, wouldn't the quality of our work lives improve if these interactions were more similar to the examples above?

Be a Mind Reader

Many times when a customer becomes angry and directs her anger at us, she is experiencing fear, concern, or even hurt. Displaying empathy or attempting to connect with what the customer is feeling puts us in a very effectual position. By understanding what the customer may be feeling rather than only observing her behavior, we can address the root of the person's actions and thereby solve any problems or deescalate any unpleasant situations.

Understanding our customers' emotional needs is a company's secret weapon in the competitive environment that is the service industry. The customer has actually told us what he wants and his requests cost us virtually nothing to deliver. Here is what all of our passengers need from us:

1. To be greeted and feel welcome

2. For us to be approachable

3. For us to be available

4. For us to have a professional image

5. To get a personal "thank you"

The rewards of using our emotional intelligence to meet the needs of our customers are innumerable.. Remember, the positive experiences created by those on the front line are what cause customers to come back.

Each time we create a positive customer experience, we leave a lasting impression in the customer's mind about us and as about our company.

Don't Take It Personally

It doesn't matter if you work for the best company in the world and have just received the Employee of the Month award for the twelfth month in a row; sometimes circumstances arise that are beyond even the best employee's control.

On occasion, customers will come to your place of employment angry and resentful due to situations that have absolutely nothing to do with you or the company you work for. These kinds of encounters can potentially mess with your mind, because they seem like a personal affront; however, resist the natural tendency to take this type of customer conduct personally. Remember, this customer doesn't even *know* you, so how can you internalize what they do or say on a personal level?

If you let them, these types of encounters can interrupt an otherwise perfect service record and negatively shape subsequent professional interactions.

When you find yourself in an unfortunate customer service experience, it is important to remember several things. First of all, some people have simply not been trained in the art of etiquette as you have. As a result, there are people out there who do not understand how to be civilized in social situations. Secondly, while they may push your patience to the extreme, these are the people who need your services the most, because they need to be exposed to a positive role model (that would be you) to serve as an example of civility and courtesy.

Additionally, people like this are often very unhappy in their own personal situations, so berating them or delivering an impromptu lecture will not improve the situation. Ultimately, you may be surprised to find that these people tend to respond best when you continue about your business as though they had never been offensive in the first place. Keep your demeanour courteous and unruffled, and you may see them mirror your conduct. Remember, it's difficult to fight with someone who refuses to throw a punch.

Play to the Crowd

Working in the customer service industry is like being an athlete playing in front of a sold-out crowd. Together, you and your co-workers are a well-oiled machine. Your customers—your paying fans—have come to watch a spectacular performance. They expect their team to be in top-notch condition, ready to give the other guys a run for their money. Even up to the final seconds before the buzzer, they expect you to come through and go for the final point. When you make it, you feel like a hero. But when you don't, you run for the therapist's couch, feeling like a failure.

But if you have truly tried your best, you cannot take failure personally. Use your emotional intelligence to deal with difficult customers, and remember that success would not feel as sweet without the occasional failure. *If you've never experienced defeat, how can you cherish victory?*

Let's face it, people are people, and when you work in customer service, you never know what you are going to get. It's a mixed bag of personalities, perceptions, and attitudes. In this sense, it may seem as though the customers have the power to make or break their own service experiences. However, you alone can make or break your own *reaction* to the customer's experience.

In reality, the ball is on your side of the court. If you are prepared and you use your emotional intelligence, you can handle difficult experiences with poise and confidence, resulting in zero damage to your self-esteem, confidence, and overall perception of your career.

Be the Voice of Experience

Customer service and customer experience are two completely different commodities. Both are important to the business sector, but in different ways.

Customer service hinges on things we can see and measure quickly. For example, do employees greet customers, do they smile, and are they competent?

Customer experience, on the other hand, is grounded in how customer service makes the customer *feel*. Many companies believe the customer experience is the key to customer satisfaction and loyalty.

Whether at Tiffany & Co., Best Buy, or McDonald's, good customer service is easy to spot, and the way it is conducted from business to business is strikingly similar. When the customer requests a certain item, the service professional brings it to him (or, in some cases, the customer serves himself). Maybe there is a greeter at the door, for example, or maybe a clerk points out the aisle where the desired item is located. The cashier or the server is pleasant and polite.

Then, once the customer has received the product or service, his expectation has been met. Often, though, there is nothing particularly special about the encounter. The request was fulfilled, and the customer received his diamond, his iPod, or his Big Mac, but nothing was done to ensure that this customer will choose to return in the future. No one employee did anything to affect him on an emotional level. The customer simply got what he asked for and nothing more.

So even after the customer has received good customer service, he can be easily swayed to go anywhere the next time he wants the item he just purchased. There is no guarantee, not even an expectation, that he will try to return to the same establishment for a repeat performance. In fact, he will probably make his next similar purchase based on price alone, because let's face it, what else does he have to look forward to?

On the other hand, customer experience is like a fine piece of art that the customer service professional can craft in an attempt to leave a lasting impression on a customer's psyche. A memorable customer experience can take place in any business, from the Mercedes Benz dealership to the corner diner. What matters is how the customer perceives the experience.

In a quality customer experience, service providers consider the client as an emotional being who is affected by the sensations around him— sights, sounds, tastes, and smells. The emotional aspect of a customer's experience varies by client, and is based on individual expectations and perceived outcome. Therefore, the employee pays close attention to, and carefully feeds, the customer's feelings and emotions.

In this ideal situation, a customer walks away feeling emotionally satisfied, and that is literally money in the bank—not only because of the likelihood that he will return for more business, but also because he will probably tell others about his positive experience—and good word of mouth is the best kind of advertising for any company.

With a positive customer experience, a customer's request has been met or exceeded. Quality service has been rendered, and the business and its employees have left a lasting impression on the customer's emotional memory.

On the flip side, what about situations when customer expectations are not met? Can a customer still walk away with a positive emotional experience? The answer is definitely *yes*.

Company cutbacks, supply and demand, or unforeseen events can conspire against the system and thwart expectations, often resulting in a negative customer experience.

A customer service employee never enjoys saying "no" to a client; however, sometimes that answer is unavoidable. The key is to learn how to say "no" or "I'm sorry," while still affecting the customer in a positive way. It's all in the delivery.

On these occasions, a responsive customer service employee is most valuable; minimal collateral damage occurs when the customer is left in the hands of a psychologically astute service provider.

Go to Your Happy Place

Airline passengers express displeasure in a wide variety of ways. They may complain or criticize, raise their voices several decibels, or spew profanity at you. You are a convenient target because, after all, you are the face that represents what is wrong with their day.

A glitch in flight plans or in other customer expectations can cause the sweetest, most docile customer to morph into something that resembles a shrieking banshee from the underworld. Worse yet, the customer may not express any discontent, but simply storm out with no intention of ever returning.

Irrespective of how the customer chooses to reveal their emotions, the method you choose to defuse the situation, and how you calm a seemingly inconsolable customer, can make all the difference in the world. If you can remain serene yet attentive, you have just initiated human communication, and they feel validated.

Communication is the key to any healthy relationship, and it's also the best-kept secret to being effective and surviving the trials and tribulations of any customer service job successfully. Why? Because communication skills are the foundation on which everything in this industry is built. We communicate through various modes, including how we dress, how we speak, and how we act. Granted, these are all exterior qualities, but they are rooted in what cannot be seen: our attitudes, our judgement, and our intellect.

Send Them to Their Happy Place

Acknowledge, Accept, and Apologize. These are the three steps you can take to turn around a negative experience. This is a subtle, yet effective psychological tactic used by successful corporations to smooth troubled waters:

> **Acknowledge.** There is no better way to refocus a negative situation than by agreeing there's an issue, because it forces the customer to switch gears. The customer, who is likely to be completely caught up in everything that went wrong with your company, probably hasn't considered the possibility that you might actually agree with him.
>
> When something goes wrong, first let the customer explain his situation and vent, if needed. Then agree with him and

acknowledge flat-out that there's a problem. In addition, you have taken the time to let him communicate something important to him. Sit quietly, hear what the client has to say, and then tell him you agree with the fact that this has been a less-than-ideal situation. I mean, really, what can the customer say if you agree with him that there is something amiss?

Once the customer has calmed down, you can provide a few comforting words to show you empathize with the situation. It's good to remind ourselves of a time when we have been in this exact situation, and if we haven't, to acknowledge that we likely will sometime in the future. In short, a little bit of empathy goes a long way.

Then update the customer frequently to assure him that you haven't forgotten about him and to let him know what's being done to remedy the situation.

This step of acknowledging the customer's feelings and concerns puts you in the valuable position of being an ally, and not the enemy.

Accept. Next, take responsibility for the issue. Obviously you are not responsible for the rain, snow, sleet, or hail that has kept your 777 grounded for the past two hours. To this customer, at this moment, however, you represent the company and everything that is right or wrong with it. Accepting responsibility simply means you are a warm body intertwined with the problem, which is exactly what they need.

Also keep in mind that you in a powerful position not only with this customer, but also with the other 199 customers within earshot. Everyone around you is waiting on pins and needles to see how you handle this potentially uncomfortable situation. By publicly acknowledging the problem and then accepting responsibility, you have let the entire plane, or hotel, or restaurant know that you are fully aware this is a rough situation and that you want to help everyone make the best of it.

In reality, they know it isn't your fault, but they do expect you to handle it like the professional that you are. In other situations, acceptance means not only saying that you or your company are responsible for the problem, but that you are also committing to resolve it.. This is what your customers and your employers really want to know: they are in the hands of a powerful and competent individual. If it is humanly possible to make the situation better, then do so. This is what everyone expects from you.

Apologize. A genuinely felt "I'm sorry" works miracles to smooth ruffled feathers. "I'm sorry" connects with your customer on an emotional level and reminds her that both of you are human. It is also a concrete manifestation of the empathy you feel toward the customer, and it reinforces your intentions to fix the problem.

Once the anger is defused, you can breathe a sigh of relief and take the next steps to creating the most positive customer experience possible.

Become Engaged

Whether you are a customer or an employee, you know the pleasures and pitfalls that come with human interaction. Many erroneously believe that employee-customer encounters do not matter because you will never see that client, flight attendant, or service representative again. It's true—maybe you won't see the person again—but you will have slews of other encounters throughout the days, weeks, and even years to come. So why not make every one of these count by using each personal encounter as a springboard for future interpersonal experiences?

As a person on this planet, you hold power over the type of interpersonal experiences you have, and you rightfully deserve and expect encounters that are positive. So here are a few simple techniques to help you get the most from your daily human interactions.

Be Long-Sighted

Don't be afraid to look people in the eye. Making eye contact, or avoiding it, speaks volumes. Eye contact is a profound form of nonverbal communication that creates an immediate first impression. When you look another person in the eye, you send the message that you feel confident in your own skin. You also let the other person know that you accept him as he is and welcome the interaction between you. This silent communication confirms that both parties are held in high esteem. We also have to realize that some cultures are uncomfortable with eye contact, so it is important to take cues from the individual.

On the other hand, failing to look another in the eye, or purposely avoiding eye contact, can send a negative message, or at least leave everyone guessing. Is this person shy or nervous? Are they hiding something? Or do they just have something better to do? This awkward moment can distract from the focus of the original purpose of the encounter: weren't you attempting to communicate? Again, depending on culture, eye contact may be held for short or longer amounts of time.

In the world of customer service, wise use of eye contact can lead both parties into a mutually beneficial relationship. People on each side of the transaction feel security in knowing that they have been heard. It is a great icebreaker before getting down to business.

Mince Your Words

Good manners and civilized communication go a long way. Choosing your words carefully shapes a person's response to your requests and may help you get what you want. At the very least, it will make your customer's service experience more enjoyable.

Consider a customer service encounter as you would any other type of encounter or introduction: know what you are going to say ahead of time. Come prepared with questions, answers, or examples, depending on the situation. State your expectations clearly; no one can read your mind. Convey options, solutions, and unforeseen pitfalls. And don't forget to factor in time. If you know you will need ten minutes to clearly explain a situation, make sure you've got it. Turn off your cell phone or pull the customer to the side, if you need to, to prevent unwanted interruptions.

Using respectful, explicit, and well-formed language accomplishes two things: it shows people that you value their time and, in turn, sends a clear message that what you have to say is important.

Mind Your Manners

These days, it seems that general communication skills and etiquette are not often considered; however, these seemingly miniscule details make a world of difference in your attitude and, ultimately, in the world around you.

How often do you say "please" and "thank you"? How often do you really look at or connect with the strangers you interact with on a daily basis? Do you call your server, your cashier, or your customers by name?

Make a conscious decision to say "please" and "thank you", and take note of the responses you get—they may surprise you. .

Take a risk and smile genuinely at the next person you see, taking the time to really look at him. How does it feel when he smiles back?

Notice how you feel inside when you present your best self to the world. Good manners help the giver as much as, or perhaps even more than, the receiver.

Here are just a few ideas for making your daily interactions more meaningful. When you are in public, ask your server his name and use it. Most customer service employees wear nametags for this reason. When you take a check or credit card from a customer, notice the name printed on it, so that when you hand the customer her purchases, you can say, "Thank you, Mrs. Johnson."

When you give or receive money, place it firmly in the recipient's hand instead of just laying it on the counter; you aren't going to get cooties from anyone, and it's a great way to connect on a personal, rather than superficial, level. People find this more personal level of interaction a welcome surprise, and often respond in kind, giving you more personal attention in return.

Another tip: treat others as equals. Butting in line could mean that you are in a terrible hurry, but more likely, it means you are an inconsiderate jackass who thinks he's more important than anyone else. If you are in an emergency, just ask the person ahead of you *politely* if you may jump ahead. The worst they can say is no. And a final word to the wise about line-jumping: don't ask someone with a mere handful of items to let you slip in front of them if you've got a whole cartload of things to purchase—that, also, is treading dangerously close to that inconsiderate jackass territory.

Finally, speak *to* people, not *at* them.

Listen.

When appropriate, tip well and often.

If you have ever worked in customer service, you know how much all of this means.

Employ Euphemisms

You have the power to set the tone for each interaction you have. For each personal encounter you experience, your attitude can work either for or against you. When you are approached by that sulky, depressed teenager or a scattered, preoccupied individual who greets you with a grunt from the other side of the counter, how do you respond?

Perhaps the kid or the scatterbrain does need to learn some respect and common courtesy, but is a lecture from you right at this very moment going to help things? Instead of "trying to teach someone a lesson," remember that we lead best by example. Also remember that the noble adage, "Treat others as you would like to be treated" pays off, especially when you are on the short end of the stick.

Finally, remember that it takes two to tango. A person may attempt to push your buttons just to see what they can get away with. It can be difficult, but do not relinquish your power to another person by letting them control your emotions. This is not a pissing contest. Use supervisors and managers as needed. This is what they are there for. Let them sort out the more complicated issues and lend you support when you find yourself at a crossroads.

Lastly, don't take mistakes personally. Mistakes are going to happen. You will order your hoagie without mayo and it will come with mayo. A customer will tell you they want the sweater in red and change their mind at the last second, swearing they requested blue all along. When the flight attendant spills your gin and tonic on your new, Italian suit, she didn't do it because she doesn't like you or because she thinks the suit is ugly ... she simply had a hard time navigating the bumpy, narrow aisle of the plane. She isn't out to get you; she does respect you; it was an accident, nothing more. Put yourself in her place; how would you feel if you accidently did the same thing to a person you were trying to impress?

Get Real

Be realistic about what you request and expect of others, and don't make promises you cannot keep. Do not make outrageous demands, and don't say things you do not mean. Be willing to let others help you as needed.

Remembering these simple rules will work wonders. Demonstrate kindness, courtesy, a little emotional intelligence-- and sit back and watch the quality of your customer service grow by leaps and bounds.

Choose Your Poison

A loyal customer in the market, Mrs. Crabbe looked like something out of a 1930s movie. Her eyes were wide with sky-blue eye shadow and her cheeks were pasty white except for two perfectly formed blood-red, quarter-sized circles. Her lips seemed to be stained a permanent shade of Pepto-Bismol pink. Her choice in clothing bordered on the eclectic; cheetah patterned boas were a common occurrence. Her hair looked as though it were coming out in clumps, and what little remained was fixed at the back of her head, having been pressed into shape, I assumed, by her pillow the night before. She always had her little dog To-Toy with her, riding high in the front of her shopping cart, yapping loudly as small dogs do at anyone who dared to walk past them. No one, not even my typically outspoken manager, dared to tell Mrs. Crabbe that dogs were not allowed in the supermarket.

She came to the store twice a week. Each time she stopped by my deli counter she bought the same thing: half of a coffee cake and a quarter pound of German potato salad. The older women I worked with scattered like cockroaches when they saw her coming, leaving me, at the tender age of seventeen, to fend off Mrs. Crabbe by myself. I suppose they figured they'd earned the right, as the older generation, to pass her on to me.

I can honestly say I hated this crazy old woman, because it seemed her life's mission was to make my life miserable. Each Friday, like clockwork, Mrs. Crabbe would come in to return half-eaten portions of the items I had sold her earlier in the week. Our conversation typically went as follows:

Mrs. Crabbe: I'm returning this coffee cake and I would like my money back; it tastes like shit.

Me (thinking): Well, some of it must have been okay because you ate most of it.

Mrs. Crabbe: I'm also returning this German potato salad. What, are you trying to kill me? It's got gasoline in it!

Me: No Mrs. Crabbe, I'm not trying to kill you, and I'm fairly certain there is no gasoline in there.

Mrs. Crabbe (screaming and thrusting the remnants of her German potato salad under my nose): Smell it!

Denying the existence of gasoline was always futile. In fact, it didn't take me long to figure out that this only infuriated her more. Eventually I relented, scooped up another quarter of a pound, and sent her on her way, but not before she smelled the new batch just to make sure it was untainted.

As usual, as soon as she got the potato salad home, it would mysteriously take on the distinct odor of gasoline, so she would return it yet again.

This went on for months, until one day, after being abandoned yet again by my co-workers, I decided to play along with her gasoline conspiracy theory. I had nothing to lose and nothing better to do. So this time when she shoved the potato salad under my nose, the scenario went a little differently.

"Yes, it does smell like gasoline," I said. "I see what you mean."

At this point, her face went blank. She apparently didn't know what to do. I panicked, thinking maybe I had pushed her too far. But then she smiled—the first smile I had ever seen escape her crusty Pepto lips.

"Yes," I replied cautiously. "I smell a distinct odor of gasoline!" I could hear giggles coming from my boss in the back room.

"What are you going to do about it?" she croaked.

"We keep the gasoline-free salad in the back," I said. "I can get you some of that if you'd like."

"Yes, please," she replied. (To the best of my knowledge, Mrs. Crabbe had never said please to anyone on the planet!)

Then, taking her unleaded German potato salad, she went on her way. From that day on, she never returned another food item so long as I packaged it up from the rear of the store. She never again accused me of trying to kill me with poisoned food.

In hindsight, it was really a simple solution: she just wanted someone to see things from her point of view. Once I agreed with her and provided service on her terms, she became easier to manage, which made my job less stressful.

As a bonus, my boss was not only appreciative, but impressed as well. And although I was the youngest person on the job, I gained a lot of respect from my co-workers—unfortunately, not enough respect to make them wait on Mrs. Crabbe!

Put It On Ice

Do you ever find yourself getting defensive when a customer is raging or being irrational? Unfortunately, negative thinking isn't going to solve anything in the long run.

Instead of conjuring up evil revenge plots or designing a voodoo doll that looks like that notorious business-class passenger, shift your mental gears into problem-solving mode. Focus on keeping your cool and defusing the situation.

Fighting fire with fire only results in burning—for all parties involved—and may cause irreparable damage to your feelings about your career and then even to the career itself. Is it worth it to let a surly customer, perhaps even a chemically imbalanced individual, to wield this much power over you? Is it worth it to let such a person jeopardize your future?

Probably not. So instead of blowing your cool, allow your inner peacemaker to take a shot at troubleshooting. You will be proud of yourself for staying in control, and odds are that the situation will resolve itself in your favor, as well as in the customer's.

Nail It

I remember an exchange I had with a contractor during the construction of a house next door to mine in Miami. Having just finished landscaping my yard, I became a little irritated when I saw construction vehicles parked on my new grass and sprinkler system. Several times, I happened to be outside when the trucks were arriving and was able to ask them to move into the street. I wasn't always so lucky, however.

One afternoon, I arrived home only to find several pickup trucks on my grass again, so I walked over and asked to speak to the contractor for a moment. I assure you, I was very pleasant. So pleasant that he appeared to have no idea that I was even unhappy; in fact, he may have thought I was about to make an offer on the house myself!

Once I had his attention, I asked him if he would mind instructing his staff not to pull onto my lawn, as I had just finished landscaping and had suffered damage to my sprinklers in the past. Without warning, he exploded. He proceeded to tell me, with plenty of expletives mixed in, that I had been nothing but a bother since they began building the house.

My first instinct was to fire back at him with some expletives of my own, but then I remembered that so much of what we learn in customer service can, and should, be applied to daily interactions, and I chose, instead, to stay calm. I took a deep breath and then quietly said to him, "I understand how you feel, *and* I want to let you know that no matter how upset I get about this situation, I will never speak to you in a disrespectful manner. I want you to be able to sell your house for the highest possible price, and I can help you by having my property look its very best. Keeping my lawn in perfect condition is my way of contributing to the successful sale of your beautiful new home."

He was stunned all right! The difference between this response and one involving profanity or insults was that I did not leave any emotional scars on him or on myself.

So many times when we just fire back at people, we leave ourselves feeling anxious and guilty for hours, days, or longer as we replay the traumatic battle over and over again in our minds. On the contrary, I was able to look back on this situation and feel a great sense of pride.

Flex Your Intellect

Do you enjoy games that test your mental agility and intellect? You are familiar with Sudoku, Rubik's Cube, and crossword puzzles, right? Well, think of your customer service job as one big brainteaser. Believe it or not, there are myriad opportunities in your everyday customer service environment to help you flex your mental muscle and fine-tune your talent for thinking strategically—in short, to help you strengthen your emotional intelligence.

Part of our emotional intelligence is learning how to take someone's behavior into account as we decide how to react. In the book *Put Your Emotional Intelligence to Work,* authors Jeff Feldman and Karl Mulle outline behaviors and the underlying feelings those behaviors represent[4]. In the example of my exchange with the contractor, his lashing out and attempting to shift the focus of our discussion to what a pain I had been was likely caused by his underlying emotion: he was probably embarrassed. So you see, his attack on me was not even a personal one. It had to do with his feelings. All he needed was a little bit of empathy from me to free him from that embarrassment so that, together, we could resolve the situation.

As you will see in the next chapter, empathy is an ingredient we can never use too much of when dealing with people.

Once you begin to think of each workday and personal encounter as a unique series of challenges to master, you'll look forward to your profession, and your life in general, because you'll have empowered yourself to bring the best you have to offer to the forefront of all of your experiences. In simpler terms, if things turn ugly, you'll gain the confidence, energy, and skill to set things right again.

Make Empathy Your Ticket

I have had the wonderful opportunity to travel around the world as I speak about Jetiquette. The meaning of Jetiquette has grown to mean more to me than ever, with each experience I have had as a customer service professional, a public speaker, and a traveller. Although I have obviously travelled a lot as an airline crewmember, using my "free" passes, I needed to travel as a fare-paying passenger to truly understand what good service means to customers. When a customer pays for something, a contract is formed in which the customer is given a good or service in exchange for payment. If the customer is satisfied with the product or service, that is fine. If the customer is satisfied enough to form some sort of an emotional connection with the company, that is great! But the only way that emotional connection can be formed is if the customer feels appreciated, valued, and recognized.

As a purser for American Airlines, I was guilty of treating valuable customers as though they were a dime a dozen. I wish I could go back now and apologize to all of them. At American, as at most airlines, the frequent-flyer program bestows an elite status on passengers who fly the most. With this status comes perks such as first-class upgrades, priority check-ins, etc., but most important is star treatment. Although later in my flight attendant career, I developed an attitude that allowed me to provide stellar service to these elite passengers, I did not know just how much they appreciated my service until I became an elite frequent flyer myself.

An important thing to remember is that the most valuable customers—those who spend more than average customers do with a company—don't start out as such. These key people usually start just by testing the waters to determine whether a company is worthy of their business. Once they discover they've made a wise decision to do business with this particular company, they will begin to turn over a higher percentage of their business to that company.

Therefore, it's important not to pigeonhole "regular" customers, because there are potential lifetime fans hidden within the masses. Everyone deserves special treatment. Patrick McCarthy, Nordstrom's all-time top-selling salesperson, epitomizes this ideal. He is notorious for his stories of customers with haggard appearances spending surprising amounts of money at the store and becoming his most loyal customers[5].

So when a loyal customer continuously patronizes a company, it's likely because that customer feels part of the business. When you consider the customers' emotional and financial contributions to the business, there is absolutely no question that they are an important component of a company's success. In fact, without these loyal patrons, the company would not exist.

Did you know that emotionally engaged customers spend 23 percent more than the average customer?[6] Think about how much you enjoy spending money at a store or with a company that you are emotionally attached to. You can tell you are emotionally attached if you feel a sense of excitement when you even think about going there. Try it!

Behave Yourself

Here's another important situation in which using a little empathy will go a long way. It is sometimes difficult to provide the best possible service when surrounded by people that have chosen not to perform up to this standard. I refer to those co-workers who drag their feet, complain about their jobs, and just have an overall negative attitude. I'm sure we've all been in a situation with this type of person; in fact, at times, I can honestly say that I have been the negative one.

One of my favorite speakers, Joe Nunziata, says that it's best to stay away from complainers[7]. I agree. It is best to distance yourself from these people whenever that "hate" starts gushing from their mouths. This doesn't mean you need to ignore them. Just politely excuse yourself and then return when everything has quieted down. Repeat when necessary, and eventually this person will get the hint.

On the flip side, remember to have empathy for complainers as well. The truth is that everyone complains, and applying empathy helps us to understand the complaining as a way for someone to reduce or alleviate frustration in certain situations.

While empathizing, you might also suggest that the complainer come up with solutions to their problems in order to make the most out of their frustration. Usually, that not only shuts them up, but in many cases, also motivates them to do some good, which gets them positive results and eventually helps them put the habitual complaining behind them. That's because once a person realizes that he can take action to change the frustrating situations, he gets a sense of empowerment that can dramatically change his outlook. I've had to let co-workers know that I really do not want to hear negatives because I really want to focus on the positive. It's also good to remind them that complaints should be accompanied by a suggested solution as well.

Even when there is little you can do to change a frustrating situation, you can still choose to change your focus to something that you do have a positive influence on. In the case of customer service, you can change your focus from complaining about long hours, to making a customer or co-worker feel good about himself.

It all starts with empathy.

Strut Your Stuff

There is no better way to get your day off to a winning start than to walk out of your house feeling marvelous about the way you look and present yourself. The self-confidence that comes with looking our personal best is not to be taken lightly. Whether or not we want to admit it, our appearance affects how we go about our day, perform in our work, and interact with others.

Did you know that a study by researchers at Princeton University in 2006 showed that within the first few seconds of meeting, we make conscious and subconscious assessments of the others based on their appearance? And then we spend most of the time that immediately follows that first assessment looking for information to substantiate our initial judgement. This can be both good news and bad, depending on that first few seconds! Why not give yourself an immediate edge by presenting your best self from the first moment of contact.

Lighten Up

Ironically, communication begins before you've even made a sound. Believe it or not, how you look communicates as much to customers as what you do and say. You've seen them, I've seen them, we've *all* seen them: I'm talking about those folks who secretly, yet sincerely, believe their everyday lives exist on a movie set, as if at any moment the Paparazzi might unexpectedly tumble out of the overhead compartment, pop up from behind a display, or lunge at them through the fitting room curtains hoping to bag that million-dollar shot. All sarcasm aside, though, looks do matter. Now, does this mean we all have to look like Aphrodite and Apollo? No, it simply means you should make the most of your God-given talents.

Do not make the mistake of letting your face, your cologne, or your jewelry mask your sparkling personality. All eyes are on you, so focus that attention on your ability and know-how and not on that ridiculous twelve-karat, pineapple-sized, faux-diamond stud earring painfully pulling on your ear lobe. I'll give you an address to mail that diamond to, though.

A billion-dollar industry can't be wrong when it comes to gracing the faces of millions of women around the world. When used appropriately, cosmetics have the uncanny ability to transform you. They may not transform you from a sallow-faced brute to a runway model, but they can bring out your strong features and help you emit your own natural beauty in a surprisingly short time and with minimal effort.

Guys can also take measures to be sure they have a well-groomed, polished look by using scrubs, masks, toners, and moisturizers to create a clean, crisp appearance. Just stop by the cosmetic counter of your favorite department store and ask for help. Soon you'll have enough know-how to begin replacing some of the more expensive products with comparable drugstore brands. Paying extra attention to your skin has the added benefit of helping you look younger. Give it a try, and you may be quickly addicted to all of the compliments you'll receive.

Use Common Scents

If looking great is a priority, then smelling great should be too. Yet, before you select that special fragrance, consider how you would respond to this particular scent in close quarters and over a long period of time. Within the confines of shared public space, there is no such thing as subtle. If someone's got BO or taken a dive into a vat of the latest *eau de toilette*, we're all going to know about it rather quickly.

In other words, try to avoid spritzing yourself from head to toe when you fly, and just stick to the basics when it comes to personal hygiene; soaps, body washes, and deodorant go a long way. Save the friskier stuff for when you've got your feet planted firmly on the ground. After all, no one wants to be trapped with someone who smells like a cheap date.

Who doesn't love the dazzle of a diamond or the glimmer of gold? Even so, it helps to be selective when choosing jewelry. Wedding rings and sentimental items never go out of style, but keep your additional pieces tasteful and limited. Try to avoid earrings that resemble your grandmother's chandelier and opt for basics like hoops or studs. When it comes to rings and bracelets, select elegant and slender designs that compliment your hand or wrist, not the gaudy baubles that make your knuckles drag on the floor.

Take Pride and Groom

These days, when it comes to hair, most men go to substantial lengths to create that signature look. Bed-head, five o'clock shadow, and the dreaded unibrow should be avoided like the plague, at least professionally. And whether you choose to keep your face fresh and smooth or lean toward the artistically inspired facial coif, keep it uncluttered. Staying trim and tidy shows that you care about your appearance and exudes confidence and good sense without being distracting. Remember, razors and tweezers are your friends; unruly nose hairs and wiry brillo-brows are not!

Talk With Your Hands

When it comes to working the friendly skies, your hands speak volumes. Keeping them scrubbed and unsullied is important. Would you want to be served by your own hands? Does a beverage nestled inside dry, cracked, rough, hang-nailed, chipped polish-encrusted fingers appeal to you? Well, it probably doesn't appeal to your customers either.

Ladies, glaring, fluorescent nail color can lead patrons to safety in case of an emergency, but that's what the exit signs and back-up generators are for! Men, there is no shame in securing an occasional manicure. With a few professional particulars, you'll have the best looking paws on the plane ... hands down!

Yes, the world can be shallow. But the reality is that, as professionals, we are judged according to how we look. Get over it. While wearing a uniform can make you feel like a clone, remember you have the most important tools to establish yourself as an individual at your disposal 24/7: your scintillating personality, your seraphic spirit, and your tough-as-nails psyche. Simply enhance your natural beauty and don't rely on the superficial maneuvers.

Hold Your Head High

The customer service industry needs your brand of talent. It is getting increasingly difficult to find people willing to go the extra mile and provide stellar service. You have the experience and talent; use these to your advantage! Consider yourself lucky because you have the best tool of the trade firmly planted between your shoulders. What more could you want?

As a person in customer service, you are developing your own brand within a brand. In fact, many customers will come to think of you when they think of the company you are working for. Who knew? *Human Sigma*, by John Fleming and Jim Asplund, shares how 70 percent of a customer's view of a company is shaped by interactions with its employees[8]. The Human Sigma methodology is a new take on customer service quality control that takes into account the variance from one interaction to another. It also places significant value on the level of customer and employee engagement, recognizing that those companies with the highest levels of both are consistently more successful.

Keep Your Focus

As customer service professionals, we have the amazing opportunity to learn on a regular basis simply by paying attention to our interactions with customers and with one another. So much of what we learn on the job equips us to navigate skilfully through the most treacherous human interactions—both personally and professionally. In this way, our on-the-job education can improve the lives of everyone.

To gain knowledge from our experiences, however, we have to keep our eyes open as we move along this journey, open to seeing the many opportunities available for learning valuable lessons.

We also have to realize that we will not discover all of this wisdom while working. Many will come to us when we are playing the part of the customers. When we go to the drugstore or the bank, we can use information we gain from taking on the customer perspective to help us better serve our own clients. From the behavior we exhibit as customers, for example, we may gain insight into why passengers act certain ways.

Do the Right Thing

We must also remember that it is never too late to go back and repair mistakes we've made; doing so helps to reinforce our learning. Perfection is not the goal, and besides, it's more personally and professionally effective to stay focused on how we make others feel than on achieving perfection.

One of my most valuable learning experiences happened when I was a prospective customer at a very popular San Francisco restaurant, Spruce. I had arrived there one night with two colleagues and no reservation. The hostess politely told me that she would do her best to get us a table, but that it would be a forty-five-minute wait and suggested we have a drink from the bar. Well, forty-five minutes came and went, and by the time I completed my second martini, I realized we were not ever going to get a table. I was disappointed and felt a little foolish for even thinking we could get a table in the first place. After all, it was a Friday night in the most happening restaurant in San Francisco.

So I told the hostess that we needed to close out our tab and get a taxi. With a genuine smile, she said she would take care of that right away. I responded with a phoney smile and a sarcastic, "Thank you." Before I knew it, we were in a cab headed off to a less popular restaurant.

A little later, I thought about how I had treated the hostess. It bothered me that I had made another person in customer service feel bad about doing her job, especially when she was obviously trying to do it well. I thought about how many times I had encountered grouchy customers and how it made me feel. I definitely didn't want to be the type of person to make someone else feel that way. How could I correct it?

At the airport the next evening, I decided the only thing left to do was to call the restaurant and apologize. Before I could finish describing myself to the hostess, she informed me that she remembered who I was. I could tell from the tone of her voice she had been emotionally scarred by my behavior and wondered whether I was about to bash her. Instead, I told her how sorry I was, that I wanted her to know she was excellent at her job, and that she had really made an impression on me. Her voice changed to excitement as she thanked me and invited me to contact her the next time I came to town so that she could arrange a table for me.

This is an example of the power our interactions have to make negative and, better yet, positive differences in people's lives. It also shows how we can use our daily interactions to help us improve ourselves and our minds. Remember, learn from your mistakes and take pride in your accomplishments.

Maintain Cabin Pressure

Finally, to learn and grow, we must open our minds to different ways of seeing and believing. If we can do that, we can free ourselves of a pattern of frustrating reactions and behaviors. James J. Mapes, author of *Quantum Leap Thinking*, describes how our own beliefs can cause us problems: "If you tend to think that the problem is 'out there,' then your thinking is the problem"[9]. In a lot of situations, we point fingers at and make accusations of others, when our frustration is actually rooted in what *we* believe.

As customer service professionals, our learning never ends. It is just that simple.

Always remember that you are a valuable asset to the customer service industry. You are worthy of your power and position; never take your ability to provide quality customer care for granted. Not everyone can do what you do for a living.

Your career literally allows you to make a difference in the world on a daily basis because you interact with large numbers of people. Use your talents wisely and relish in the fact that you have the power to go wherever you want to go and influence hundreds, if not thousands, of people in a unique and meaningful way. Use what you know about exceptional customer service to carry over into your personal philosophy of life.

The sky's the limit because you truly deserve to love what you do.

Bibliography

1. Judith M. Bardwick, PhD ; *One Foot Out the Door*, p. 21

2. Jonathan Tisch; *Chocolates on the Pillow Aren't Enough*, p. 202

3. Jonathan Tisch; *Chocolates on the Pillow Aren't Enough*

4. Jeff Feldman and Karl Mulle; *Put Your Emotional Intelligence to Work*, p. 48

5. Robert Spector and Patrick McCarthy; *The Nordstrom Way to Customer Service* Excellence

6. John Fleming and Jim Asplund; *Human Sigma*

7. Joe Nunziata; *Spiritual Selling*, p. 71

8. John Fleming and Jim Asplund, *Human Sigma*

9. James Mapes; *Quantum Leap Thinking*, p. 189

For more information about Gailen David and Jetiquette, please visit www.skysteward.com.

NOTES

www.ingramcontent.com/pod-product-compliance
Lightning Source LLC
Chambersburg PA
CBHW021016180526
45163CB00005B/1976